APPRENTICESHIP PROGRAM FOR MOS OF AIR TRAFFIC CONTROL NAVIGATIONAL AIDS TECHNICIAN

WORK EXPERIENCE LOG

APPRENTICE NAME_____

DEPARTMENT OF THE NAVY
HEADQUARTERS UNITED STATES MARINE CORPS
WASHINGTON, D.C. 20380

PCN 100 013413 00

ERRATUM

to

NAVMC 2724

WORK EXPERIENCE LOG

AIR TRAFFIC CONTROL NAVIGATIONAL AIDS TECHNICIAN

1.   Change the PCN shown at the bottom of the cover page from "PCN 100 0131412 CO" to 1'PCN 100   0131413 00."

DISTRIBUTION: 2000(1O)/2020(1OO)/2030(35)/2069 (200)/
                    Less 2105/2132/2133/21314/2135/21145/2157/
                    2169/2191.   3700/7501/7508(10)

Copy to: TRI(50)

TABLE OF CONTENTS

INTRODUCTION

APPRENTICESHIP

Apprenticeship is training for jobs in technical trades that require special skills and knowledge. It involves technical schooling and planned on-the-job training under supervision. For young workers desiring to gain a skilled occupation, the apprenticeship program provides a step-by-step program of instruction and on-the-job training. This program will lead to advance standing in the technical skill or trade you have chosen.

The USMC Apprenticeship Program provides you with the opportunity to enhance your advancement in your chosen skill area while on active duty. As you progress in your training in the Marine Corps and master the skills required of your trade, you will have the mastered skills recorded in your log. The apprenticeship program allows you to make your work experience in the Marine Corps count twice. First, to fulfill your active duty obligation in a productive manner. Second, to provide you with a usable skill if you should decide to return to civilian life. By having documented proof of Marine Corps schooling and work experience, you should be able to compete and qualify for a better job at higher pay.

Most apprenticeship terms range from 1 to 4 years, depending upon the trade involved. To master a particular trade requires: (1) Learning all or most of the skills of the trade; (2) perfecting each specific skill, (3) bringing each skill up to the speed and accuracy required of the job; and (4) learning to use specific skills in combination with other skills.

MARINE CORPS APPRENTICESHIP PROGRAM

The purpose of establishing the Marine Corps Apprenticeship Program is to provide Marine Corps commanders an opportunity to implement programs of apprenticeship for military personnel in occupations closely related to and applicable to private industry needs and requirements. Marine Corps school training and experience in the field will, if properly documented, satisfy private industry requirements for the training of apprentices in nationally recognized apprenticeable occupations.

The ultimate objective of the United States Marine Corps Apprenticeship Program is to provide registered certification of an individual Marine's skilled craft occupational training. The program has been designed to achieve recognition for Marines equal to their civilian counterparts.

Registration of the National Apprenticeship Standards for the United States Marine Corps with the Bureau of Apprenticeship and Training, U.S. Department of Labor, is beneficial to the Marine Corps, to individual Marines, and to private industry, management, and labor. Acceptance of U.S. Marine Corps apprentices as skilled crafts-workers by private industry, management, and labor will enhance Marines employment opportunities as veterans, shorten the term of private industry apprenticeship through the award of appropriate credit for previous military training experience, and provide a source of registered skilled personnel to meet national manpower requirements.

THE AIR TRAFFIC NAVIGATIONAL AIDS TECHNICIAN APPRENTICESHIP PROGRAM

The purpose of this pamphlet is to announce the United States Marine Corps Apprenticeship Program for the trade of Air Traffic Navigational Aids Technician.

Policies and procedures for participation in the program are contained in MCO 1550.22.

Marines holding a primary or secondary 5952/5955 MOSs and are serving in that MOS may participate in the program.

This is an 8000 hour program which leads to a certification of journeyman in the trade of Air Traffic Navigational Aids Technician by the U.S. Department of Labor. Participation in the program is voluntary, and no membership in labor unions or professional associations is required. The work process schedule and schedule of related instruction are outlined on pages 8 through 13. The purpose of the work process schedule and the schedule of related instruction is as indicated below:

> The work process schedule reflects categories of work experience required by Marine apprentices to qualify as Journeyman Air Traffic Navigational Aids Technician.

> The schedule of related instruction identifies courses which are available to Marine apprentices to satisfy the 144 hours of annual related instruction required for completion of the program.

Marines eligible for the program may enroll by contacting the Unit or Base Education Officer who will assist in the preparation of the application.

Apprentice logs and instructions on their use will be provided by the Education Officer at the time of registration. Marine apprentices will be required to maintain their own log sheets on a <u>daily</u> basis. Log entries must be verified by the Marine apprentice's immediate supervisor on a <u>weekly</u> basis.

Marines who have partially completed an approved Federal or State registered civilian apprenticeship will be awarded credit within the constraints of the individual apprenticeship training program standards. Each training hour successfully completed in the occupation involved will be awarded credit upon presentation of authenticated documentation. Marines serving beyond their initial enlistment are considered career Marines, and may make application for the apprenticeship program in order to be certified as having completed an apprentice program. Career Marine apprentices must complete the same requirements as the first-term apprentice except that they will be given credit for one-half the hours required for the specific apprenticeship program in which they are enrolled provided their previous enlistment was served in an MOS applicable to the relevant apprenticeship program for which applying.

Organized related instruction for all United States Marine Corps apprentices will be defined by the individual apprenticeship program standards. Such related instruction will be provided on an hour-per-year basis, or the total hours may be achieved through the successful completion of a multi-week training course for the apprenticeable occupation involved at any United States Marine Corps training school, or other service school (Army, Navy, etc.) providing such training.

Upon successful completion of apprenticeship training and experience requirements as prescribed by individual apprenticeship program standards, the apprentice will submit a request via the chain of command, accompanied by a letter from the appropriate commander or education officer, to the Office of National Industry Promotion, Bureau of Apprenticeship and Training, U.S. Department of Labor, Washington, D.C. 20213, for issuance of a Certificate of Completion of Apprenticeship (Enclosure 10). The Bureau of Apprenticeship and Training will issue all Certificates of Completion of Apprenticeship to the individual through Headquarters, U.S. Marine Corps (Code TRI) to the appropriate commander.

NATIONAL APPRENTICESHIP STANDARDS

FOR

THE UNITED STATES MARINE CORPS

Developed by Headquarters, United States Marine Corps, Washington, D.C.,
with the assistance of the Bureau of Apprenticeship and Training,
Employment and Training Administration, United States Department of Labor,
Washington, D.C.

AUTHORITY

National Apprenticeship Standards for the United States Marine Corps are established by authority of:

W. GRAHAM CLAYTOR JR.
Secretary of the Navy

RAY MARSHALL
Secretary, United States Department of Labor

LOUIS H. WILSON
Commandant of the Marine Corps

Registered as incorporating the basic standards recommended by the Bureau of Apprenticeship and Training, Employment and Training Administration, United States Department of Labor.

HUGH C. MURPHY
Administrator
**Bureau of Apprenticeship and Training
Employment and Training Administration**

Registration Number N-91040   DATE July 7, 1977

5

DEFINITIONS

1. EMPLOYER....................The United States Marine Corps.

2. PROGRAM SPONSOR..............Commanding Officer.
   Marine Aviation Training Support
   Group-90, Naval Air Technical
   Training Center, Naval Air Station,
   Memphis, Millington, Tennessee 38054

3. NATIONAL APPRENTICESHIP
   STANDARDS....................The entire document which embodies
   the procedures for the selection
   and training of Marine Corps apprentices and sets forth all the
   conditions associated therewith,
   including training on-the-job,
   related technical instruction, and
   administrative responsibilities.

4. WORK EXPERIENCE LOG..........A book issued to each registered
   apprentice identifying the occu-
   pation, work process training
   schedule, hours allocated to each
   training task increment in the
   work process schedule, and
   supervisory certification requirements.

5. APPRENTICE...................Any individual who is on active
   duty in the U.S. Marine Corps, meets
   entry age requirements, performs
   assignments that include training in
   an apprenticeable occupation and who
   is registered with the Bureau of
   Apprenticeship and Training,
   U.S. Department of Labor,
   Washington, D.C.

6. REGISTRATION AGENCY..........The Bureau of Apprenticeship and
   Training, U.S. Department of
   Labor, Washington, D.C.

7. WORK PROCESS SCHEDULE.......An outline of work procedures which
   specifies the required supervised
   work experience, training on-the-
   job, and the approximate time to
   be spent in each major process.

8. SCHEDULE OF RELATED INSTRUCTION.... Organized, related and supplemental instruction necessary to provide apprentices with knowledge in technical subjects related to the trade. The instruction may include supervised correspondence or self-study courses, as approved by law or by policy of the registration agency. A minimum of 144 hours each year of apprenticeship training is required. It may also include resident instruction at a DOD or civilian school. Normally, a minimum of 144 hours annually is required. However resident, formal schooling can satisfy total requirements for related instruction if over 360 hours are attained.

WORK PROCESS SCHEDULE FOR THE TRADE OF
AIR TRAFFIC CONTROL NAVIGATIONAL AIDS TECHNICIAN

1.   Participant Designation. Marines working in the Military Occupational Specialty (MOS) 5952 and 5955 are authorized to participate in this program.

2.   Job Description. Assembles and disassembles system, preparing them either for operation or shipment, as applicable. Surveys, sites and installs TACANS, homing beacons and instrument landing systems in accordance with appropriate directions. Performs required adjustments on TACANS, homing beacons and instrument landing systems and record the accomplishment in accordance with appropriate directives. Tests adjusts and aligns the systems for proper operation using internal and external test equipment. Diagnoses and isolates malfunctions to the faulty part. Removes and replaces faulty parts, verifies that the fault has been corrected. Identifies parts required to be replaced by use of appropriate publications and prepares requisitions to obtain parts from the supply system. Records corrective maintenance on maintenance action forms in accordance with appropriate publications. Interprets schematics, wiring diagrams and technical data contained in associated publications to maintain TACANS, homing beacons and instrument landing systems. Observes and applies proper safety procedures with respect to system operation and maintenance. Makes authorized modifications/field changes to navigational aid systems. Trains personnel in the proper procedure for maintaining navigational aid systems. Prepares lesson guides for the units technical training program for navigational aids systems.

A.   Orientation to navigational aids Systems, such as UHF/VHF   1600
omni directional beacons, tacan, instrument landing systems,
test equipment, operations, maintenance and repair techniques,
and processes.

     1.   Apply shop practices for the proper use, maintenance,
care, and storage of test equipment.

     2.   Employ safety practices as outlined in established pro-
cedures pertaining to voltage and moving mechanical parts.

     3.   Develop work shop and component equipment cleaning
techniques.

     4.   Observe an experienced technician and participate in
identification, use, care, and storage of hand tools and
specialized trade tools.

B.   Trouble-shoot navigational aids systems using standard   2000
diagnostic methods, procedures, and test equipment.

     1.   Study circuit diagrams and check system alignments.

     2.   Interpret circuit and schematic diagrams, technical
literature, and related documents.

     3.   Identify the location and purpose of components, sub-
assemblies, and auxiliary equipment.

     4.   Determine malfunctions and the locations of mechanical
and electrical/electronic components.

     5.   Determine waveform and voltage amplification.

     6.   Determine faulty components by direct current measure-
ments, AC and DC voltage measurements, and resistance
measurements.

C.   Inspect and repair electrical/electronic and mechanical   2000
navigational aid equipment and components.

     1.   Utilize and follow blueprints, diagrams, and
manufacturer's specifications.

     2.   Compute voltage, amperage, and resistance factors.

     3.   Test faulty equipment components and circuits.

     4.   Disassemble malfunctioning equipment and repair or
replace faulty components.

5. Inspect, adjust, and align components.

6. Prepare and file maintenance records.

D. Final test operate equipment with standard and specialized   2000
test equipment.

   1. Multimedia

   2. Vacuum tube voltmeter

   3. Digital voltmeter

   4. Oscilloscope

   5. Tube checker

   6. Transistor checker

   7. Signal generator

   8. Pulse generator

   9. Frequency counter

  10. Wattmeters

  11. Spectrum analyzer

  12. Built in test equipment

  13. Other associated test equipment

E. Perform organizational and preventive maintenance as   400
required.

   1. Perform visual inspection

   2. Clean machine, filters, equipment, test equipment and
tools.

   3. Lubricate per requirements and as necessary.

TOTAL   8000

SECHEDULE OF RELATED INSTRUCTION

COURSE NUMBER	COURSE TITLE	RESIDENT SCHOOL	HOURS CREDIT
A-1OO-O1eo	Basic Electricity and Electronics	NATTC/Memphis	145
A-1OO-2013	Avionics "A" Schools	NATTC/Memphis	450
C-103-2026	Mini Component Repair Course	NATTC/Memphis	40
C-103-2020	Air Traffic Control Navigational Aids Repair Course	NATTC/Memphis	646
C-103-2030	Air Traffic Control Navigational Aids Technician Course	NATTC/Memphis	1310
A-102-0045	Tacan Maintenance, Electronic Tech	SERSCOLCOM/GLKS	376

COURSE NUMBER	COURSE TITLE	CORRESPONDENT SCHOOL	HOURS CREDIT
28.6	Fundamentals of Digital Logic	MCI	20
CDC 32652C	Navigation and ECM Systems	ECI	120

<u>INSTRUCTIONS FOR COMPLETING WORK EXPERIENCE LOG</u>

This pamphlet is issued to each registered apprentice and identifies the occupation, work process training schedules, hours allocated to each training task increment in the work process schedule and supervisory certification requirement.

1. <u>Marine applicant will</u>:

    a. Complete the apprentice registration application (enclosure (1) in triplicate. Forward one copy to CMC (Code TRI), one copy placed in Marine's Service Record Book (SRB), and the third copy is to be retained by the Education Officer.

        (1) Submit the application to the commanding officer or his authorized representative.

        (2) Obtain work experience log, which includes the Work Experience Functions. Obtain one year's supply (12 copies) of the Apprentice Work Experience Hourly Record, (enclosure (2)) from the commanding officer or education officer.

        (3) Complete the Personal History Form, (enclosure (3)) and forward to CMC (Code TRI) with enclosure (1), if necessary.

        (4) Complete Military Education, (enclosure (4)), and forward a certified copy to CMC (Code TRI) with enclosure (1), if necessary.

        (5) Complete Civilian Education, (enclosure (5)), with certification from the Marine's Service Record Book and forward to CMC (Code TRI) with enclosure (1), if necessary.

        (6) Maintain Military Assignment, (enclosure (6).

        (7) Civilian Occupation, (enclosure 7), if applicable submit statement to program sponsor on employer letterhead, giving length of employment, position held, and manner of performance.

    b. Career oriented apprentice Marines must complete the same requirements as the first-term apprentice except that they will be given credit for only half the hours required for the specific program in which they are enrolled. This is provided their previous enlistment was served in an MOS applicable to the relevant apprenticeship program for which they are applying.

        (1) A certified photocopy of enclosure (6) of the work log will be forwarded with the registration application to CMC (Code TRI).

(2) The commanding officer or his designated representative will assign credit hours for previous work experience in accordance with MCO 1550.22 and mark accordingly block 16 of enclosure (1).

2. <u>Procedures for Recording Hourly Work Experience</u>

a. Daily Record. Daily entries will be made by the apprentice.

b. Weekly certification by supervisor: Weekly certification will be completed by the shop chief for whom the Marine works.

c. Consolidation/Certification on Month/Yearly recapitulation: The signature line of the work experience hourly record will be signed by the commanding officer or his representative. This report will reflect the entries for the monthly work experience, enclosure (8) of work experience log.

3. <u>Semiannual Progress Interview</u>

a. Report to your unit Education Officer within 5 to 8 months after date of this application and twice a year thereafter. Enclosure (9) will be completed and forwarded to CMC (Code TRI).

b. The purpose of the interview is to determine the status of the apprentice and to certify a photocopy of the last hourly record of work experience.

c. The Commanding Officer or Education Officer/authorized representative will sign the Apprentice Progress/Status Report (enclosure (9)).

4. <u>Interruption of Assignment</u>

a. Rifle Range/Leave. Record on the experience hourly record the days away from regular assigned duty.

b. Separation from Active Duty. Status report will be submitted to CMC (Code TRI) identifying the Marine as being discharged. Upon request, CMC will forward the records to Bureau of Apprenticeship and Training in the Marine's home state of record.

c. Sickness and hospitalization. Recorded by day on the Apprentice Work Hourly Report.

d. Voluntary Disenrollment. An apprentice must request suspension or cancellation. Suspension retains the apprentice in a temporary status for no more than one year. A request for suspension may be submitted via the Commanding Officer for CMC (Code TRI) by the apprentice. Cancellation removes the apprentice from the apprenticeship program. A request for cancellation requires signature of the apprentice's Commanding Officer or Education Officer.

5. <u>Documentation Required to Validate Related Instruction</u>. Certification of completion of transcript of grades will be used to award credit hours toward completion of the apprenticeship program.

6. <u>Loss of Work Experience Log</u>

    a. Request a reissue of a blank log from the Education Officer of your command.

    b. Request CMC to furnish data available in your records to bring the log up-to-date.

APPRENTICE REGISTRATION APPLICATION (1500)
HAVMC 11013 (3-77)
SM: 6.30-04-804-4800 U.'1: SM

1. Print or type.
2. Prepare in triplicate.
3. Forward original and one copy to CMC (Code OTTE).
4. Apprentice retains one copy in Work Experience Log.

PRIVACY ACT NOTIFICATION

Under the authority of Title 5, U.S. Code, Section 301, the information regarding your former and present active military service, educational background and present personal data is requested in order to review and evaluate your qualifications for the Department of Labor apprenticeship program for active-duty Marine Corps personnel. Your Social Security Number is used for purposes of individual identification. This information will be retained by the Commandant of the Marine Corps (Code OTTE) and by the Bureau of Apprenticeship and Training, U.S. Department of Labor, and will not be divulged without your written authorization to anyone other than Headquarters Marine Corps and Department of Labor personnel involved with administration of this program. You are not required to provide this information, however, failure to do so may result in your not being registered for an apprenticeable trade.

APPLICANT INFORMATION

1. NAME (last, first, middle)	2. SSN	3. DATE OF BIRTH (Day, Month, Year)	4. SEX ☐ MALE ☐ FEMALE

5. RACE/ETHNIC GROUP
☐ CAUCASIAN/WHITE ☐ NEGRO/BLACK ☐ AMERICAN INDIAN ☐ SPANISH AMERICAN ☐ ORIENTAL ☐ INFORMATION NOT AVAILABLE ☐ NOT ELSEWHERE CLASSIFIED

6. NAME AND LOCATION OF HIGH SCHOOL FROM WHICH GRADUATED	OR, STATE AND DATE OF GED EQUIVALENCY

7. Did you serve on active duty on or after 5 August 1964 and before 8 May 1975? ☐ YES ☐ NO	8. HOME OF RECORD (State)

9. APPRENTICEABLE TRADE FOR REGISTRATION (Give complete title)	10. DOT CODE FOR APPRENTICEABLE TRADE	11. APPRENTICE PROGRAM

I agree to report to the education officer within 5 to 8 months after date of this application and twice a year thereafter. I understand that my registration is voluntary and that registration does not guarantee work or duty assignments appropriate to my apprenticeship. I have read and understand the Privacy Act Statement.

12. Signature of applicant _____   13. Date _____

TO BE FILLED IN BY APPLICANT'S COMMANDING OFFICER OR EDUCATION OFFICER

TO: Commandant of the Marine Corps (Code OTTE), Headquarters U.S. Marine Corps, Washington, D.C. 20380

14. FROM

15. Total hours required for term of apprenticeship   _____ hours

16. Hours credit given for previous work experience   (-) _____ hours

17. Total hours remaining for term of apprenticeship   _____ hours

18. COMMENTS (if any)

19. SIGNATURE OF REGISTRAR	20. TITLE	21. DATE
The applicant has been counseled as to the conditions and requirements of the apprenticeship. Signature _____		

Enclosure (1)   15

Item No.

    1: Self-explanatory.

    2. Enter Social Security Number.   Example: 399-03-6433

    3. Enter date of birth: Day, Month, Year.

    4. Self-explanatory.

    5. Self-explanatory.

    6. Self-explanatory.

    7. A check "X's in the YES block signifies that the registrant is regarded as a Viet Nam veteran by the Department of Labor.

    8. Enter name of state which the registrant calls home.

    9. Enter long title of apprenticeable trade. Example: Camera Repairer. Entries are limited to those apprenticeships authorized by the Commandant of the Marine Corps.

    10. Enter 9-digit DOT code which matches the apprenticeable trade entered in Item 9. The Work Processes Schedule indicates this code.

    11. No entry required.

    12. Self-explanatory.

    13. Self-explanatory.

    14. Enter name and address of command forwarding application.

    15. Enter total term of the apprenticeship (required hours for completion). Example: 6000. The Work Processes Schedule indicates the total term of the apprenticeship.

    16. Enter hours of creditable work experience completed prior to registration, if any. A registrant may be credited with 1000 hours of previous work experience for each full year that his/her service record validates assignment to an MOS applicable to the apprenticeable trade. Applicable MOSs, if any, are listed at the bottom of the Work Processes Schedule for each authorized apprenticeable trade. However, credit for previous work experience completed prior to registration cannot exceed more than 50% of the term of the apprenticeship. Therefore, no more than 3000 hours of previous work experience can be credited to a 6000-hour apprenticeship. Portions or fractions of years of work experience will not be credited.

    17. Enter the difference between Item 15 and Item 16. This difference Is the number of work experience hours which must be completed by the apprentice.

    18. Enter any comments regarding previous work experience, future assignment or next duty, or further explanation of any above item. Entry not mandatory.

    19. Signature of commanding officer, education officer, or his authorized representative.

    20. Title of registrar who signed Item 19.

    21. Enter date that Item 19 was signed. This will be the effective beginning date of the apprenticeship.

APPRENTICE WORK EXPERIENCE HOURLY RECORD (1500)
·NAVMC 11015 (3-77)
SN: 0000-00-006-6840 U/I: SH

APPRENTICE NAME *(Last, first, middle)*

1. Print legibly.
2. Enter completed hours daily or weekly.
3. Have Supervisor verify hours at the end of each week.
4. Keep this record in your Work Experience Log.

WEEK OF	DATE FROM						DATE TO						SIGNATURE & TITLE OF SUPERVISOR												

DAY	LETTERS IDENTIFIED IN WORK PROCESSES SCHEDULE																										TOTAL HOURS
	A	B	C	D	E	F	G	H	I	J	K	L	M	N	O	P	Q	R	S	T	U	V	W	X	Y	Z	
SUN																											
MON																											
TUES																											
WED																											
THURS																											
FRI																											
SAT																											
TOTAL HOURS																											

WEEK OF	DATE FROM						DATE TO						SIGNATURE & TITLE OF SUPERVISOR												

DAY	LETTERS IDENTIFIED IN WORK PROCESSES SCHEDULE																										TOTAL HOURS
	A	B	C	D	E	F	G	H	I	J	K	L	M	N	O	P	Q	R	S	T	U	V	W	X	Y	Z	
SUN																											
MON																											
TUES																											
WED																											
THURS																											
FRI																											
SAT																											
TOTAL HOURS																											

WEEK OF	DATE FROM						DATE TO						SIGNATURE & TITLE OF SUPERVISOR												

DAY	LETTERS IDENTIFIED IN WORK PROCESSES SCHEDULE																										TOTAL HOURS
	A	B	C	D	E	F	G	H	I	J	K	L	M	N	O	P	Q	R	S	T	U	V	W	X	Y	Z	
SUN																											
MON																											
TUES																											
WED																											
THURS																											
FRI																											
SAT																											
TOTAL HOURS																											

WEEK OF	DATE FROM					DATE TO						SIGNATURE & TITLE OF SUPERVISOR															

DAY	LETTERS IDENTIFIED IN WORK PROCESSES SCHEDULE																										TOTAL HOURS
	A	B	C	D	E	F	G	H	I	J	K	L	M	N	O	P	Q	R	S	T	U	V	W	X	Y	Z	
SUN																											
MON																											
TUES																											
WED																											
THURS																											
FRI																											
SAT																											
TOTAL HOURS																											

WEEK OF	DATE FROM					DATE TO						SIGNATURE & TITLE OF SUPERVISOR															

DAY	LETTERS IDENTIFIED IN WORK PROCESSES SCHEDULE																										TOTAL HOURS
	A	B	C	D	E	F	G	H	I	J	K	L	M	N	O	P	Q	R	S	T	U	V	W	X	Y	Z	
SUN																											
MON																											
TUES																											
WED																											
THURS																											
FRI																											
SAT																											
TOTAL HOURS																											

SIGNATURE & TITLE	DATE

PERSONAL HISTORY

LAST NAME	FIRST NAME	MIDDLE INT.
RANK	SOCIAL SECURITY NUMBER	DATE OF BIRTH DAY/MONTH/YEAR
PLACE OF BIRTH		
PERMANENT HOME OF RECORD		

SIGNATURE OF APPRENTICE   DATE

_____   _____

19

Enclosure (3)

MILITARY EDUCATION

COURSE TITLE	LOCATION	LENGTH;	FROM:	TO:

TOTAL EDUCUCATION HOURS_____	FIRST YEAR HRS._____	SECOND YEAR HRS._____	THIRD YEAR HRS._____
	CERTIFIED: _____	CERTIFIED: _____	CERTIFIED: _____

CIVILIAN EDUCATION

HIGH SCHOOL OR GED/	NAME, ADDRESS, ZIP CODE/ GRAD. DATE
COLLEGE OR GED/	NAME, ADDRESS, ZIP CODE/ GRAD. DATE
VOCATIONAL SCHOOLS	
LIST ALL SEPARATE COURSES TAKEN	
LIST ALL OTHER SPECIALIZED TRAINING NOT COVERED ABOVE	

MILITARY ASSIGNMENT

UNIT	ADDRESS	FROM	TO	DUTY ASSIGNMENT

Enclosure (6)

CIVILIAN OCCUPATION

LIST ALL CENTRAL OFFICE REPAIRER RELATED EMPLOYMENT COVERING THE LAST TEN (10) YEARS.		
FIRM, NAME AND ADDRESS	NO. OF YEARS	POSITION HELD

WORK EXPERIENCE FOR _____
(YEAR)

	Jan	Feb	Mar	Apr	May	Jun	Jul	Aug	Sep	Oct	Nov	Dec	Total For Yr	Int
A														
B														
C														
D														
E														
F														
G														
H														
I														
J														
K														
L														
M														
N														
O														
P														
Q														
R														
S														
T														
U														
V														

A. TOOLS
B. MATERIALS
C. SYSTEMS TERMINOLOGY
D. DISTRIBUTING FRAMES
E. SHIP CLEANING TECHNIQUES
F. SAFETY PRACTICES
G. MAINTEANCE ADMINISTRATION
H. TELEPHONE SWITCHING
I. ELECTRICAL STEPPING SWITCHES
J. LINE CONDITIONING EQUIPMENT
K. INTERCEPT EQUIPMENT

L. AUTOVON TRUCK CIRCUIT EQUIPMENT
M. INSTALLATION PRACTICES
N. CABLE COLOR CODES
O. WIRE WRAPPING
P. TESTING PROCEDURES
Q. TROUBLESHOOTING
R. SOLDERING GUN/HAND TOOLS
S. REQUISITIONING
T. ELECTRICAL SWITCHING SYSTEMS
U. AUTOMATIC SWITCHING SYSTEMS
V. SWITCHBOARDS

_____
CERTIFICATION OFFICIAL

_____
TITLE

APPRENTICE PROGRESS/STATUS REPORT (1500)
NAVMC 11014 (3-77)
SN: 0C00-00-006-6840 U/I:SH

1. Print or type.
2. Prepare in triplicate.
3. Forward original and one copy to CMC (Code OTTE) with attached
photo of last Hourly Record of Work Experience.
4. Apprentice retains one copy in Work Experience Log.

PRIVACY ACT NOTIFICATION

Under the authority of Title S, U.S. Code, Section 301, the information regarding your former and present military service, educational background and present personal data is requested for purposes of individual identification. This information will be retained by the Commandant of the Marine Corps (Code OTTE) and by the Bureau of Apprenticeship and Training, U.S. Department of Labor and will not be divulged without your written authorization to anyone other than Headquarters Marine Corps and Department of Labor personnel involved with the administration of the apprenticeship program. You are not required to provide this information; however, failure to do so may result in cancellation of your registration in an apprenticeable trade.

To be filled in by Apprentice or official in accordance with instructions on reverse side.

1. NAME OF APPRENTICE (Last, first, middle)	2. SSN	3. SEX ☐ MALE ☐ FEMALE

4. RACE/ETHNIC GROUP
☐ CAUCASIAN/ WHITE ☐ NEGRO/ BLACK ☐ AMERICAN INDIAN ☐ SPANISH AMERICAN ☐ ORIENTAL ☐ INFORMATION NOT AVAILABLE ☐ NOT ELSEWHERE CLASSIFIED

5. Did you serve on active duty on or after 5 August 1964 and before 8 May 1975? ☐ YES ☐ NO	6. HOME OF RECORD (State)

7. Apprenticeable Trade in Which Registered	8. Total Hours for Term	9. Hrs. Preregistration Experience	10. Hrs. Completed Since Registration	11. Hours Remaining

TO: Commandant of the Marine Corps (Code OTTE), Headquarters U.S. Marine Corps, Washington, D.C. 20380

12. FROM (Activity submitting report)

ACTION REQUESTED

(check one)

13. Please suspend registration for the apprentice named above for the reason(s) checked below:

a. ☐ Orders to light duty

b. ☐ Nature of current assignment prohibits work in apprenticeable trade for one year or less

c. ☐ Hospitalization

d. ☐ Operational commitments prevent reporting for progress interview

14. ☐ Please lift the suspension of registration for the apprentice named above effective: _____
(Date)

15. ☐ Please cancel the registration of the apprentice named above for the reason(s) checked below:

a. ☐ Commanding officer's prerogative

b. ☐ Discharge or release to inactive duty

c. ☐ Termination of work experience for one year or more

d. ☐ Death

e. ☐ Failure to report for twice-a-year apprentice progress interview

f. ☐ Personal request of apprentice

16. ☐ The apprentice named above has completed all required hours of work experience in all areas of the apprentice trade. A "Certificate of Apprenticeship Completion" is requested.

17. SIGNATURE OF APPRENTICE	18. DATE

19. SIGNATURE AND TITLE OF OFFICIAL	20. DATE

Enclosure (9)   25

INSTRUCTIONS FOR APPRENTICE PROGRESS/STATUS REPORT

Item No.

1. Self-explanatory.

2. Enter Social Security Number. Example: 399.03.6433.

3. Self-explanatory.

4. Self-explanatory. Must agree with Item 5 of apprentice registration.

5. Entry must agree with Item 7 of apprentice registration.

6. Enter name of state which the apprentice calls home.

7. Enter long title of apprenticeable trade. Example: Camera Repairer.

ITEMS 8.9,10, and 11 NOT REQUIRED IF SUSPENSION (Item 13) OR CANCELLATION (Item 15) IS REQUESTED.

8. Enter total term of apprenticeship as indicated on Work Processes Schedule. Must agree with Item 15 of "Apprentice Registration Application."

9. Enter number of verified hours of work experience completed prior to registration. Must agree with Item 16 of "Apprentice Registration Application."

10. Enter cumulative number of hours of work experience completed as a registered apprentice. Attach reproduced copy (photostat or xerox) of every "Work Experience Hourly Record" which shows hours completed since last report.

11. Add Item 9 and Item 10 and subtract total from Item 8. Enter result in Item 11.

12. Name and address of activity from which report is submitted.

13. Check if this is a request for suspension. Suspension retains the apprentice in a temporary inactive status for no more than one year. Request for suspension requires signature of apprentice in Item 17. A request for a suspension may be mailed directly to Commandant of the Marine Corps by apprentice. No suspension will be carried longer than one year.

14. Check here if reason for suspension no longer applies. A request for lifting suspension requires signature of apprentice in Item 17 and signature of Commanding Officer or Education Officer in Item 19.

15. Check here is this is a request for cancellation. Cancellation removes the apprentice from the apprenticeship program. A request for cancellation requires signature of Commanding Officer or Education Officer in Item 19.

16. Check if apprentice has completed all required work experience, both grand total of hours and total hours in each skill area. A check in this block must be supported by final entries in Items 8, 9,10 and 11, plus a produced copy of the "Work Experience Hourly Record" completed since the last apprentice progress interview or report. Hours of verified work experience completed before registration (Item 9), if any, will be distributed equally among the skill area of the trade. A check in this block requires signatures in Item 17 and Item 19.

17. Signature of apprentice required for Items 6, 9, 10, 11, 13, 14,15f and 16.

18. Date in which signature of apprentice is affixed in Item 17.

19. Signature of commanding officer or education officer submitting report required for Items 8,9,10,11, 13, 14, 15a and 15f.

20. Date on which signature in Item 19 is affixed.

Certificate of Completion of Apprenticeship

United States Department of Labor

Bureau of Apprenticeship and Training

This is to certify that

has completed an apprenticeship in the trade of

SAMPLE

in accordance with the standards recommended by the

Federal Committee on Apprenticeship

_____
SECRETARY OF LABOR

_____
William F. Kelling
ASSISTANT SECRETARY FOR MANPOWER

_____
Hugh C. Murphy
BUREAU ADMINISTRATOR

DATE _____

Enclosure (10)